Jalsaghar

Jalsaghar

STEFFEN HORSTMANN

PARTRIDGE

To order additional copies of this book, contact
Partridge India
000 800 10062 62
orders.india@partridgepublishing.com

www.partridgepublishing.com/india

Horstmann, Steffen.

Jalsaghar/Steffen Horstmann. 1st ed.

*

The ghazals herein, often as different versions, have appeared in the following publications, and are reprinted with permission: *The Aurorean, Blue Unicorn, Candelabrum, Common Ground Review, Contemporary Ghazals, Contemporary Rhyme, The Criterion, Das Literarisch, Free State Review, The Ghazal Page, HazMat Review, Hurricane Review, The Indian Review, Ishaan, Istanbul Literary Review, Knot Magazine, Life and Legends, Louisiana Literature, Lynx, The Lyric, Mad Swirl, Meridian Anthology, Mobius, The Morning Dew Review, The Neovictorian, Oyez Review, Pebble Lake Review, Pegasus, Poem, Raintown Review, Recursive Angel, The Red Fez, Taj Mahal Review, Texas Poetry Journal, Tiferet, Unlikely Stories, Up the Staircase Quarterly,* and *Xavier House Review.*

"The Sands," "[Absences assume shadows that graze in the outer dark]," and "Bladed Light" appeared in *Contemporary Ghazals: An Anthology,* edited by R.W. Watkins (Nocturnal Iris, 2014).

Seek the beloved of both worlds to hold in your embrace.
~ Ghalib

Your feet bleed, Faiz, something surely will bloom
as you water the desert simply by walking through it.
~ Faiz Ahmed Faiz

CONTENTS

FOREWORD

Jalsaghar: A World of Ghazals

The world of Steffen Horstmann's *Jalsaghar* is global and familiar, yet somehow loosened from specific political/geographical/historical references. For instance, in the opening couplet of "Houses:"

> Houses in which bombs left empty spaces.
> Their shattered mirrors haunted with faces.

One could describe these ghazals as depicting a shattering world, "haunted with faces."

From its origins in Arabic, the ghazal migrated to other languages, notably Farsi and Urdu, but many others as well. Now, the ghazal is becoming naturalized as a form in English poetry. For those not familiar with the conventions of the Urdu ghazal, two important ones are: both lines of the first couplet and the second line of each succeeding couplet end with the same word or brief phrase. Just before this refrain, there is a word that rhymes with the words preceding the refrain in the other lines. Common variations include using only one of these devices or using near rhymes or variations on the word in the refrain.

Steffen mostly uses the traditional Persian/Urdu ghazal form, and uses it well. His lines tend to be shorter than often found in English ghazals, many running 8-10 syllables and four or five accents. The following couplet, from "Ghazal (Late at Night)," illustrates Steffen's use of the form. (This is an opening couplet.)

> I wander streets we would walk at night,
> Passing cafés where we'd talk at night.

Another convention of the Urdu ghazal is that the last couplet contains the poet's name or pen-name. Steffen doesn't utilize this convention much; a pronoun often serves that purpose. Here is the last couplet from "Whom We Call Ishmael:"

> We search for him whose words have guided us ~
> The Belovéd ~ whom we call Ishmael tonight.

Adapting a verse form with such specific conventions into English can be difficult. Steffen follows the conventions effectively, and he departs from them equally effectively. Using a rhyme with no refrain allows him to collate and overlap images, as in the last two couplets of "Broken Ghazal:"

We once sped on rails to autumnal lands.
Now clouds travel the routes of those defunct trains.

My hands memorize your hourglass waist ...
Slow winds pass through distant sands, sifting grains.

This ghazal exemplifies Steffen's use of startling imagery, speaking of love in a variety of settings from pastoral to urban.

Another variation in English ghazals is three-line stanzas (tercets instead of couplets). Robert Bly devised this form, and several poets have written fine ghazals with it. Steffen's "Light Streams Through the Stained Glass Madonna," is an example of his use of light-imagery to express transcendent emotions and experiences.

A firm convention of the ghazal is that each couplet is considered an independent poem and the theme should jump and shift between them. Even though these discontinuities are important, there is also the tradition of ghazals with sustained, continuous themes. One of these in *Jalsaghar* is "Whom We Call Ishmael," a portrayal of social-political-spiritual catastrophe. As a whole, the ghazal depicts an apocalypse with ghosts, executions, falling angels, tornadoes, and (suddenly) The Belovéd, who is now called Ishmael. Since each couplet is separate, this poem definitely feels like a ghazal; yet the scene is built up like a montage of photographs, or stills from a movie.

"Whom We Call Ishmael" depicts a world of violence and shadows. The title not only recalls the opening of Moby Dick but also the traditional descent of the Arabic tribes from Abraham's son by Hagar, Ishmael. Rejection, exile, familial alienation resonate with other imagery of this ghazal. The last line, as well as the title, also alludes to Agha Shahid Ali's posthumous collection of ghazals, *Call Me Ishmael Tonight*. Steffen works this rich texture of allusions into a poem that will make perfect sense even to the reader who "gets" none of the allusions.

"[Translucent hummingbirds emanating]": the monorhyme of this ghazal floats and flickers like a hummingbird, as the poem depicts exotic scenes from across the world: Italy, Russia, India, Japan, Mexico, in a shifting overlay of references. It is well worth the reader's time to do a little Web searching to find the multiple meanings of the words involved.

A Foreword is not the place to do detailed prosodic analyses of the poems in the collection, so I've selected one line from an early poem as an example of Steffen's melodic ear:

Words whir like insects from books in a pyre,

Listen to the relations of the vowels in "Words whir" and notice how "books" picks up the "c" in insects, and then how the closing "r" reflects "Words whir." Similar aspects can be seen in any of the lines of these ghazals. Part of the pleasure is hearing them in your own reading.

Steffen's meter is especially admirable ~ or rhythm, which is perhaps the better term as being more inclusive of the features of the language that make it a poem. Many of his ghazals use iambic pentameter adroitly, always expressively united with the imagery and meaning of the lines.

Another formal feature of these ghazals is condensed syntax. This is not the artificial syntax of "poetry" using an old-fashioned language with syntactic inversions and other tricks to get the meter and rhyme to work. No, this feature slows the pace of reading and draws attention to dynamism of the imagery. One example, the first couplet of "Ghazal of the Black Water:"

> Beneath trees shadows pool like black water.
> Ships spin in vortexes gales fuel in black water.

The second line uses both elision and condensation. Here is an expanded version which I offer hoping to clarify his method. My additions are in square brackets.

> Ships spin in vortexes [that are] fuel[ed by] gales in black water.

Both a relative clause and a passive voice (the words in brackets) are omitted to make the line more powerful, more intense, more musical.

Steffen Horstmann's ghazals illuminate the form's potential in English. He has been devoted to the study of the ghazal's development over the centuries and has stayed current regarding its adoption into English poetry. As a result, his ghazals are well-grounded in the traditions of both English poetry and the ghazal.

Gene Doty

Editor, *The Ghazal Page*

I

IN YOUR COUNTRY

The Sands

Caravans traverse expanses of shifting sands,
Where dunes migrate as clouds of drifting sands.

Water in a basin is sequined with starlight
That shimmers through veils of drifting sands.

Arabian stallions are shadows glimpsed
In a burnished haze of drifting sands.

Icy mountains sparkle in heat waves
That ripple above streams of shifting sands.

The currents of gales become vipers
Slithering wildly through shifting sands.

Forever

Do you seek, like Jonah, to be elusive forever ~
To live like an ascetic, reclusive forever?

You traversed deserts & abide in a mirage,
Within the shade of a fig & olive forever.

The temple scribe said you were fated to stray
In radiant absence, as wind lisps its narrative forever.

Sand rises around you, a volatile vacuum ~ O escape
To the mind's habitable star, fugitive forever.

In a vision you emerge from an emerald sea, immersed
In the light that pours through a cloud's sieve forever.

Shahid, I left you sleeping in a bed of light ~ knowing
It was I you were destined to forgive forever.

[How the bronze light of the equinox]

How the bronze light of the equinox
Gilds walls where boxers shadowbox.

How djinns mine black diamonds
Embedded in phosphorous rocks.

How fine dust glints on gold bars
Stacked in Fort Knox.

How an arrow's flight emulates
Stillness in Zeno's paradox.

How an aurora forms when phoenixes
Rise from fuming pyres in flocks.

How writhing flames are shedded
From the billowing cloaks of Nox.

How the auras of minute rainbows
Emanate from the plumage of peacocks.

How translucent pollen swarms
In meadows of saxifrage & phlox.

How the pattern of light & shade
Alters in aisles of swaying hemlocks.

How snowflakes teem like particles,
Camouflaging the Arctic fox.

How the metallic ticking reverberates
In a dream of Dali's melting clocks.

The Riptides

Kelp clouds surface in surging riptides,
Clotting with krill in merging riptides.

Oil fires discharge coils of blue smoke
Spinning in drafts from emerging riptides.

Like light dancing in jade water, schools
Of yellowtail meld in merging riptides.

With nets enmeshed, caravels revolve
In a vortex formed by merging riptides.

Snaking gales flail fog & are subsumed
In the vacuum of converging riptides.

Gyres of air slung off a cyclone's tip
Thresh mist risen from surging riptides.

Drifts of sand-hazed light leap swells
That collide in surging riptides.

Winds skim an inlet's pool & spin
In spools above merging riptides.

Kites are ensnared in air funnels
Rising from converging riptides.

[Incense lingers in a tomb where falcons]

Incense lingers in a tomb where falcons
Are embossed on Heer's coffin of light.

On Layla's gown Majnoon's reflection
Wavers in each burnished sequin of light.

From Zabarvan Shiva observes planets teem
Like dust-motes whirling in a margin of light.

Begum Akhtar clothes notes in her voice's silk
As she sings from a palanquin of light.

Hieroglyphs on pyramids depict spectral vortexes
As portals traced to the origin of light.

Darting bulbuls fashion spherical nests
In apricot groves tended by a djinn of light.

By a candle's glow Faiz scratches *Zindan-Nama*
On a prison wall that gleams like a bulletin of light.

Stars convulse in Krishna's mirror
As the glass radiates with a skin of light.

Gales billow clouds that shed phantasms
Arrayed in a pearled muslin of light.

Shiva meditates within lucent clouds
Flowing above a mountain of light.

[Sprinting djinns cast fleet shadows around you]

Sprinting djinns cast fleet shadows around you,
Forming a black vortex that flows around you.

Moths whirred through webs in torch-lit ruins
As wraiths like twisting smoke rose around you.

A nebula's kaleidoscope is infused with starlight
That forms brief paisleys in shadows around you.

Phosphorous galaxies blaze in the kiln of auroras
As a bonfire's flames cast dancing shadows around you.

You had woken in the rubble of a minaret when from
Smoking pyres flocks of phoenixes rose around you.

As clouds are bursting with the moon's vermilion light
Wind-stripped trees cast cruciform shadows around you.

In the marble corridors of tombs mystics chant sutras ~
Shrill voices ringing in torrents of echoes around you.

Circling flocks of Persian falcons create maelstroms
In clouds whipping downward to form tornadoes around you.

As a bladed moon lit the ruins of a Roman arena
The armored spectres of gladiators rose around you.

Shards of light burst from a daemon's crystal,
Casting minute prisms & rainbows around you.

A dream of silk spinning from the cocoons of moths ~
The white shroud a needle of light sews around you.

Variation on a Theme by Dylan Thomas

A razed city's ruins jackals will scour.
The cluster of stars a black hole will devour.

A Buddha's statue smashed with sledgehammers,
Its head in the rubble of a fallen tower.

But you speak of sprigs risen in cool ash
With the force of the green fuse that drives the flower.

But you recount winged-seeds cast
By winds fueled with a turbine's power.

Celestial debris laced with shards
Of planets thrashed in a meteor shower.

Nights turbulent with wraiths
Screeching in a wind-wrecked bower.

But you note how kernels of grain can germinate in dust
With the force of the green fuse that drives the flower.

But you speak of how suns combust
To assert light & light's power.

Today

A helix of flames spiraled in your eyes today,
As a soothsayer spoke of your demise today.

Beneath Thracian tombs defiled by Romans
Djinns scour crypts seething with flies today.

Mystics decipher koans whispered
In zephyrs rife with lisps & sighs today.

Plumes of smoke are roiling above pyres
From where flocks of phoenixes rise today.

Clans of nomads are possessed by demons
Sages were dispatched to exorcise today.

Cassandra dreams of ships gliding on waves of fire ~
An omen of war the sea's repose belies today.

A wraith's shrieks reverberate through caverns
In an echo the raving wind amplifies today.

The immense shadows of soaring wings melt
As condors are subsumed in the sunrise today.

The litanies of prophets are echoing in caves
As whirlwinds form in Elijah's eyes today.

The Steelhead

... reedy beaches where the steelhead ran.
~ Robert Haas

Skiffs race along reedy beaches where the steelhead ran,
Through fog-shrouded reaches where the steelhead ran.

Gales bent trees into sickles, were laced with echoes
Of a seahawk's screeches where the steelhead ran.

A lighthouse's beam is a sparkling blade slicing through
The emerald waters of beaches where the steelhead ran.

Sunrise strikes channels where gulls circle above trawlers
Dragging nets through deep reaches where the steelhead ran.

On drenched ramparts statues stand like sentries watching
The coast a tidal flood breaches, where the steelhead ran.

The Coast of Dungarvan

Foreboding omens came over the land. There were
excessive whirlwinds and lightning storms.
Then the ravaging of heathen men…
~ 11th century Anglo-Saxon chronicle

Where bats swarm in howling grottos.
Where dust-devils rove rutted verges.

Where banshees surge from seething shadows.
Where hooded monks chant dirges.

Where tide pools swirl vortexes.
Where lightning forms a flailing tree.

Where a funnel cloud is the nexus
Between the sky & the Celtic Sea.

The galloping fires & unburied dead ~
When Vikings raided the coast of Dungarvan.

The spikes of lances raised severed heads,
Staked in the sands on the coast of Dungarvan.

The reaches where bees danced in bleached skulls
Wreathed in seaweed on the coast of Dungarvan.

An incantatory echo the wind culls
From a sibyl's chant on the coast of Dungarvan.

Where snakes slithered into the sea & became currents.
Where cloaked figures slide through fog as it wavers.

Where lightning pierces the sky with tridents.
Where in the wind a sibyl's voice quavers.

[Salamanders swarm along the stream in your Japanese garden]

... of all the taboos of the century, I had to fall in love with you.
Later, the salamanders swarmed along the stream in your Japanese garden.
~ David St. John

Salamanders swarm along the stream in your Japanese garden,
Near sunlit shallows where minnows teem in your Japanese garden.

Plum petals form a delicate shroud on a samurai's shrine,
His body levitates from a pond like steam in your Japanese garden.

You watch lotus-shaped clouds transform into faces of deities ~
Nestled beneath willows (rapt in a dream) in your Japanese garden.

Hummingbirds hover before a mirror, charmed by their reflection.
Butterflies spiral in a breeze's slipstream in your Japanese garden.

Pearls embedded in a geisha's embroidered gown glisten by candlelight.
She reads Bashō & appraises her diamond's gleam in your Japanese garden.

Silence suffused with the sensation of expectancy, an aesthetic of space
Awaiting its occupant (a latent theme) in your Japanese garden.

Bonsai saplings, golden abacus, cherry trees, marble tiger ~
Lavished with the grace of an Empress's esteem ~ in your Japanese garden.

Dream of transformation you become ~ a cloud of mist lit from within
Dissolves as light leaks from an expanding seam in your Japanese garden.

Wind through grasses is the voice of a sage reciting haiku, uttered
Subtly within the breadth of a daydream in your Japanese garden.

Variation on a Theme by James Merrill

Waves of scudding clouds flood the night at Sandover.
Plane trees emit auras of white light at Sandover.

From a gramophone the chords of a ruminative suite
Waft through an empty ballroom tonight at Sandover.

Sleek tulips skirt a vined wall stenciled
With silver leaves in perpetual flight at Sandover.

A paper boat is moored with string to a lotus blossom
As wind riffles an ascending dragon-kite at Sandover.

Mirrors in the salon duplicate a queen's diamond,
Its rays flooding glass with shattered light at Sandover.

Turkish bees & emerald hummingbirds hover
Amid roses, lavender & white, at Sandover.

The winter garden is an empire of ice-sculptures
Illuminated by stars shedding blue light at Sandover.

Above an azure bay Venus is a jewel studding
The prismatic fire of twilight at Sandover.

Moths flutter through rooms of sheeted furniture, hasten
A storm of motes in the dusty light at Sandover.

I dream it restored, that rosebrick manor in the Hamptons.
The driveway is glass sparkling with light at Sandover.

JM's jotted lines are pressed into a table's grain ~
Excerpts of scripts from *The Changing Light at Sandover*.

The Rages

Words whir like insects from books in a pyre,
Swarming in smoke as burning pages rage.

Suns resplendent with gold coronas blaze
With fires that through galactic ages rage.

The swirls of Jupiter's cyclonic storms burst
In prismatic fires that through ages rage.

In the Gobi golden whirlwinds laced
With the voices of chanting sages rage.

Screeches & demonic voices emitted
From The Necronomicon's pages rage.

Wings flail amid raucous cackles
As frenzied ravens in their cages rage.

[Absences assume shadows that graze in the outer dark]

Absences assume shadows that graze in the outer dark.
Faces float in mists a zephyr sways in the outer dark.

Hypnotic rain falls in spirals, pavements thrum
As you mull in a daze in the outer dark.

Crickets tick to sparks flaring in grasses, dust wavers
With the crackling of a blaze in the outer dark.

Waves splash stones off the jetty, a palm tree dances
With its shadow as it sways in the outer dark.

Through latticed smoke phantasms shimmer
Like an auroral blaze in the outer dark.

In a pond's mist a geisha's ghost bows, you lean
To hear what her whisper conveys in the outer dark.

Dense ivy sprawls over desiccated hedgerows
That once formed a maze in the outer dark.

The stone tombs of ascetics shelter winds
That rave of forays in the outer dark.

A pulsating cloud of fireflies drifts
Like a roaming haze in the outer dark.

Wraiths formed of smoke are lit by sparks
A roiling pyre sprays in the outer dark.

On the temple grounds breezes chant koans
As a bodhisattva prays in the outer dark.

In Your Country

Whirlwinds teem amid monoliths built
Over centuries by slaves in your country.

On coastal plains the sky is a sea surging
With clouds shaped like waves in your country.

The iridescent plumage of nocturnal birds gleams
When an oceanic wind raves in your country.

Kings are entombed in icy chambers sealed
In a labyrinth of caves in your country.

Seething funnel clouds surge through wastes
Occupied by warring enclaves in your country.

The sun throbbing like a heart evaporates
Blue mists flowing from caves in your country.

Sages summon rain with the percussion
Of timbrels & claves in your country.

Voices of massacred nomads stir in the dust
Of their hurried graves in your country.

Groves of Empress trees burn as a phoenix
Propelled by thermals raves in your country.

The radiating light of the firmament
Bursts into indigo waves in your country.

[Coastal gales thresh a sunlit field of sugarcane]

Coastal gales thresh a sunlit field of sugarcane,
Swaying stalks doused with rain dissolving into light.

The scirocco crossing valleys mimics a train,
Spews sandy exhaust like rain dissolving into light.

Winds heaved from mountains steer a hurricane
Seaward, form spirals of rain dissolving into light.

Merging clouds shape the head of a stallion ~ its mane
Billows, shimmers with rain dissolving into light.

Grazing rows of corn, the wings of a landing biplane
Blaze with the sheen of rain dissolving into light.

Breezes stir, the shrill rasps of cicadas wane.
Leaves tremble, glazed with rain dissolving into light.

Amid foxtail poppies are gold as grain,
& cactus glossed with rain dissolving into light.

The spreading web of a cracked windowpane
Bears drops of rain dissolving into light.

Rocks sprout wings, become vultures circling a plain.
A nomad sleeps in shade, his dream of rain dissolving into light.

[A defunct factory, its windows become faces]

A defunct factory, its windows become faces
Witnessing the flight of each stone that smashes through them.

Empty beach houses ~ to which the monsoon has sent
(As its precursor) a knifing wind that slashes through them.

Spectres whose footsteps are sand rushing across bare floors ~
As the beacon of an unearthly light flashes through them.

You opened doors of smoke to Hell's swept expanses,
With furnaces of wind blowing ashes through them.

Simooms tend the sacred ruins of extinct tribes, repel
Intruders with a whipping gale that thrashes through them.

Bullet-laced walls thick with the ivy of executions succumb
To the grinding wheels of a tank that smashes through them.

Patrols stationed at barricaded checkpoints
Forebode every bomb-wired car that crashes through them.

Stallions are subdued by confinement in corrals,
& the whip that sends the thrust of its lashes through them.

In the Dockyards

Caulking irons sound against hulls in the dockyards,
As trash fires are circled by gulls in the dockyards.

Commuter trains glide along the towering heaps
Of scrap-metal embedded with skulls in the dockyards.

Plankings rustle with rats when breezes disperse
Whispers in the eventide lulls in the dockyards.

Kerosene rainbows swirl in puddles that shimmer
With light from the portals of hulls in the dockyards.

Within a gale's wash of notes is a tune
The flute of a reed culls in the dockyards.

Alleys glisten with shattered glass, echoing
With the screeches of gulls in the dockyards.

[I knelt before dolmens & a cloud rose over me]

I knelt before dolmens & a cloud rose over me.
The wheeling shore gulls shrieked echoes over me.

The surf heaves, funnel clouds bisect a rainbow
As a veil of spinning sand blows over me.

Tridents of lightning stoke rising fires.
Trees lash their trunks as smoke flows over me.

Grass on bluffs silvered with frosted dew
Gives rise to icy fog that flows over me.

I sleep beneath trees ~ the wind tangled in their branches ~
Nestled in cold quilts the dark throws over me.

Skies fill with birds departing barren nations ~
Forming nets of shadows, flying in rows over me.

Voices emanate from a surge of flashing foam
As bonfires cast dancing shadows over me.

Swirling debris swarms like locusts,
Propelled by colliding tornadoes over me.

I dream of a luminous white shroud
A needle of golden light sews over me.

[Clouds roil as a Shango drum echoes in the Nile delta]

Clouds roil as a Shango drum echoes in the Nile delta.
A sunbeam emits lightning-pierced rainbows in the Nile delta.

The reeds are rustic flutes a zephyr tunes, stirring sands
That hiss like cobras along the shallows in the Nile delta.

In the dry flats vacant canoes are shrouded with webs
Fine as mist (tattooed with black widows) in the Nile delta.

A crescent moon dissolves in an estuary's pool of blue light
As wraiths mimic the voices of pharaohs in the Nile delta.

Petals of African violets drift through windblown fog
& sand, sealed by dew to stalks of yarrows in the Nile delta.

Slivers of lightning moved like spiders over the Mediterranean Sea
When from a maelstrom's vortex cyclones rose in the Nile delta.

Charms rattle in a shaman's fist as wind along the shore
Thrashes trees (rousing panthers from shadows) in the Nile delta.

Stars crown citadels at twilight, shimmering in a vista
With racing skiffs a lone cloud follows in the Nile delta.

Shroud of Leaves

Air funnels form a twisting cloud of leaves,
Camouflaging graves with a shroud of leaves.

An arced blaze of autumnal light bursts
Through sieves in a swirling cloud of leaves.

A tornado's blast of whipping torrents hurl
Sparrows through a whirling cloud of leaves.

At Verdun winds writhing with smoke heaved
Upon corpses in trenches a shroud of leaves.

Whispering sutras, the circling breezes fashion
For a samurai's grave a shroud of leaves.

[Misted in sand, a woman wearing a gold sari]

Misted in sand, a woman wearing a gold sari
Dissolves in a sea of blistering dunes.

Light on a bullet-torn wall forms a brief paisley,
Alters to a map charting a sea of blistering dunes.

Figs will ripen to a tint of dark honey
In an oasis amid a sea of blistering dunes.

Clouds are ships sent from the ports of Tripoli,
Vaporizing over a sea of blistering dunes.

A black galleon with the figurehead of Kali
Patrols the sky above a sea of blistering dunes.

Ruins of a Crusader fortress in western Galilee
Are engulfed by sand in a sea of blistering dunes.

The recurring mirage of a radiant estuary
Taunts wayfarers in a sea of blistering dunes.

Spiraled yucca flowers bloom in a Joshua tree
On a sparse plain before a sea of blistering dunes.

Pyramids of fire rise in the dreams of Nefertari,
Are subsumed in a turbulent sea of blistering dunes.

Rain-shadow mountains surround the Gobi,
Confine whirlwinds in a sea of blistering dunes.

In an oasis garden dew anoints a crimson poppy
On a trellis in view of a sea of blistering dunes.

[You were entranced in the embrace of your destroyer]

You were entranced in the embrace of your destroyer,
Unwittingly caressing the face of your destroyer.

An inverted crucifix centered in her eyes gleamed
Like a diamond & lit the face of your destroyer.

Hers is the pestilent kiss of a chilled-lipped goddess ~
Implying of the subtler grace of your destroyer.

Flames form a face in fires of the Apocalypse ~
Features smoke is swift to retrace, of your destroyer.

Thunderheads roil in the depths of her mirrors.
Light flickers, revealing the face of your destroyer.

Guardian of sepulchers sealed in djinn-infested caverns ~
Twilit domain (in the hills of Thrace) of your destroyer.

In caves of cobwebbed relics dead oracles speak
From the throat of a sacred vase, of your destroyer.

Statuesque shape-shifter, her tongue addressing your ear ~
Serene whispers, in the embrace of your destroyer.

She is Kali, Venus, Medusa, Athena, Artemis ...
Wearing all expressions at once, the face of your destroyer.

You were entranced in the embrace of your destroyer,
Unwittingly caressing the face of your destroyer.

The Wind Sings in its Whirling

Death, be a blessing on the stranger
who sees the unseen more clearly
than a reality that is no longer real.
~ Mahmoud Darwish

Listen to how the wind sings in its whirling,
With leaves fluttering like wings in its whirling.

Guide me now, Lord, through the wastes
Of whistling sand that stings in its whirling.

Rumors of an oasis are whispered in flowing mist,
The murmurs of hidden springs in its whirling.

Lead me to your world, my final refuge.
Find me out in chaos of dust & storms swirling.

A dervish veers through an abandoned castle,
Laced with voices of dead kings in its whirling.

An Angel in a shawl of gleaming dark
Tempts me along a path with shadows unfurling.

I listen for a stillness within the fury,
Veiled in the wind as it sings in its whirling.

Wake me to your world, its unclouded night.
Soothe me with its soft light pearling.

Gusts lift a nomad's tent pitched in the ruins,
Vanishing in the wind as it sings in its whirling.

Listen to how the wind sings in its whirling,
With leaves fluttering like wings in its whirling.

As it Turns

The wind reads a prayer wheel as it turns,
Renders a sacred appeal as it turns.

The air fluent as with a dancer's motion,
Sound like the clicking of a heel as it turns.

Tonight the moon emits the sheen
Of a turbine's steel as it turns.

A priest in seated meditation does not hear
The wind reading a prayer wheel as it turns.

A hummingbird bows with a geisha's precision ~
Slight body the mist will conceal as it turns.

Outside the temple of the bodhisattvas
The wind reads a prayer wheel as it turns.

II

THE MANIKARNIKA GHAT

The Epoch of Whirlwinds

This is the epoch of whirlwinds
That ascend & burn.

When the spectres of Crusaders
From Byzantine campaigns return.

When the mullahs of Samarkand
Prophesy Tamerlane's return.

When the cherub of Eden
Heralds Cain's return.

This is the epoch of whirlwinds
That ascend & burn.

When the emanations of Kali
Wheeling from hurricanes return.

When the circular fires in clouds
Above the Tingri plains return.

When through Andean passes
The phantom trains return.

This is the epoch of whirlwinds
That ascend & burn.

When cloaked Horsemen
Riding stallions with fiery manes return.

When Aachen's bishops divine
Charlemagne's return.

When the priests of Avalon
Foretell Gawain's return.

This is the epoch of whirlwinds
That ascend & burn.

When from white thunderheads
The luminous rains return.

When the sands of sciroccos
In veils of shimmering grains return.

When Gregorian friars
Predict Montaigne's return.

This is the epoch of whirlwinds
That ascend & burn.

When Marian apparitions
Prefigure Saint Germain's return.

When the Celtic sibyls
Foresee Igraine's return.

When the Cardinal of Toulon
Envisions Duquesne's return.

This is the epoch of whirlwinds
That ascend & burn.

[The thunderclaps of chariot cavalries]

The thunderclaps of chariot cavalries
Routed in the Peloponnesian war persist.

The knocks made by wind hurling rocks
Against a citadel's massive door persist.

The screeches of wraiths reverberating
Within a torch-lit corridor persist.

Voices whispering in the churning
Dust on a castle's floor persist.

Prisms emitted from crystals lodged
In shards of cobalt ore persist.

The muffled chants of phantasms
Traversing an icy moor persist.

The howls of skulls formed of smoke
From Mauna Loa's volcanic core persist.

Winds roaring in the tombs of gladiators
Massacred in the Cimbrian war persist.

The echoes of Circe raving
On a desolate shore persist.

Bladed Light

Arjuna's arrows are rays of bladed light,
Streaming fluid trails of cascaded light.

Wraiths rove caves brandishing lances
Fashioned from beams of bladed light.

Beads of dew shine in willows like pearls
In Ophelia's tresses of braided light.

The white arcs of comets sizzle within
An aurora's kiln of flame-shaded light.

Jupiter mirrored in the Ganges exudes
Iridescent streams of cascaded light.

Sea winds form as Iphigenia's silhouette
Dissolves in a ring of faded light.

Icy labyrinths are lit by crystals
Casting ivory rays of bladed light.

Fluted curtains of rain billow
In mirages of brocaded light.

The Manikarnika Ghat

Mynah birds burst from a cloud of ash that billows
From pyres on the Manikarnika ghat.

Jasmine incense swirls in a fuming gust that blows
From pyres on the Manikarnika ghat.

Moths with flaming wings whirled in smoke that rose
From pyres on the Manikarnika ghat.

The apparitions of gazelles cast leaping shadows
From pyres on the Manikarnika ghat.

Sparks pulsate in latticed smoke that flows
From pyres on the Manikarnika ghat.

Rings of embers convulsed as phoenixes rose
From pyres on the Manikarnika ghat.

Chanted sutras are heard in crackling echoes
From pyres on the Manikarnika ghat.

Through curtains of cobalt flames Shiva rose
From pyres on the Manikarnika ghat.

[Radiant mica swirling]

Radiant mica swirling
In the Seine accumulates.

Pollen swarming above fields
Of burnished grain accumulates.

Reeling debris ensnared
In a hurricane accumulates.

Frozen dew shrouding stalks
Of sugarcane accumulates.

Blue dust billowing on the steppes
Of the Ukraine accumulates.

Within saffron clouds
Incandescent rain accumulates.

Bleached driftwood petrifying
On a coastal plain accumulates.

Iridescent oil bubbling
On a Siberian plain accumulates.

Phosphorescent sand on the reefs
Of Kwajalen accumulates.

Smoke funneling from the engine
Of a diesel train accumulates.

Ashen soot on the shrouded
Shield of Gawain accumulates.

A collage of leaves
In a wind-swept lane accumulates.

Glinting ash propelled
From volcanic terrain accumulates.

Beaded ice on a mustang's
Mane accumulates.

Frost clouding a shadowed
Pane accumulates.

[The dark of crevices]

The dark of crevices
Shadows crept into.

The veils of smoke
Seething sparks leapt into.

The torch-lit labyrinths
Roving winds swept into.

Roses sewn on the shawl
Juliet wept into.

[Translucent hummingbirds emanating]

Translucent hummingbirds emanating
From the diadem of Demara.

Light stitching paisleys
Into the clouds of Carrara.

Silhouettes rising in mists
From hot springs in Sagara.

Liquid mirrors undulating
In the palace halls of Samara.

The dance of spectral light
Within The Wheel of Samsara.

A monarch's chrysalis sealed
By rain to the branch of a jarrah.

Lotus petals swirling
In the wake of a shikara.

Green lightning flailing upward
From the dolmens of Connemara.

Lemon roses carpeting
The avenues of Guadalajara.

Scripture chanted from *The Gemara*.
Gems pulsing in Parvati's tiara.

Gold chalices in the tombs of Zara.
Sciroccos rising from the sands of Mara.

Stony Mesas

Roaming mists expel an aroma
Of myrrh on the stony mesas.

From within the cages of tumbleweeds
Silver crickets chirr on the stony mesas.

An Apache shaman emanates from glinting
Sands zephyrs stir on the stony mesas.

Through lacerating wind-funnels kestrals
& nightjars skirr on the stony mesas.

Wasps speckled with golden pollen scour
Sprawling larkspur on the stony mesas.

Creosote bushes combust with sparks
That pulsate & whir on the stony mesas.

Solar Fire

Phosphorescent comets spin like wheels in a solar fire.
A black vortex of whirling meteors reels in a solar fire.

Machetes of lightning slice lava clouds as shock waves
Burst in currents that slither like eels in a solar fire.

Oceans of white flames emit pentagrams of light
That convulse & revolve like wheels in a solar fire.

Variation on a Theme by Izumi Kyoka

Red of the sun, white of the beach, green of the waves.
Catamarans are subsumed in the sheen of the waves.

Seahorses swirl in the vacuum of a frilled shark's wake.
Nets hoisted onto dhows retain the sheen of the waves.

Schools of krill curl in silver bands, manta rays
Are billowing shadows within the green of the waves.

Circular gales corral the ghosts of blue whales
Dissolving like clouds in the sheen of the waves.

Buoys toss in snaking channels where the trade wind raves.
Red of the sun, white of the beach, green of the waves.

Note: The first and last line of this ghazal is the final sentence in "One Day in Spring," a short story by Izumi Kyoka (1873-1939).

Onyx Moon in a Sea of Light

Sparks crackling from the script
Of a Turkic rune in a sea of light.

Moroccan caravans traversing
A silver dune in a sea of light.

The lucent scirocco roiling
Like a typhoon in a sea of light.

Winged scarabs emerging
From a cloudy cocoon in a sea of light.

Layla's vision of the tomb
Of Majnoon in a sea of light.

The white vortex wheeling
Like a monsoon in a sea of light.

The radiant chariot
Of Neptune in a sea of light.

Ahab's plummeting harpoon
In a sea of light.

The melting sphere
Of an onyx moon in a sea of light.

III

THE DIVA OF JALSAGHAR

The Diva of Jalsaghar

Crystal chalices are shattered
By the voice of Begum Akhtar.

Sutras rise in calligraphy
From the palms of Begum Akhtar.

& palace mirrors liquefy, rippling
With the image of Begum Akhtar.

& a raga floats, visible as smoke,
From the lips of Begum Akhtar.

She is lotus-shaped clouds
Shading the pavilions of Charikar.

She is mist camouflaging elephants
In the sandalwood groves of Bihar.

She is wind piping notes
Through a flute on a sandbar.

Phosphorous gems radiate
In the diadem of Begum Akhtar.

Himalayas blaze with auras
Within the gaze of Begum Akhtar.

& wraiths rise from the Blue Nile,
Dissolving in the skies of Sennar.

& rainbows blossom from light
Swelling in the estuaries of Qatar.

She is the surf of the Arabian Sea.
She is the languid flight of the nightjar.

She is the monsoon's vortex of rain.
She is light exploding within a star.

She is the voice that issues from wind
Turning pages of The Zohar.

& she sings of the luminous
Minarets of the Charminar.

& she sings of the white fires
Blooming from the corona of a star.

& she sings of phoenixes ascending
The ashen rubble of Srinagar.

& she sings of bulbuls
Bursting from the throat of Attar.

& she sings of the rivers of Babylon
Blazing with the face of Ishtar.

& she sings of winged-seeds whirling
Through the temple courtyards of Shalimar.

& she sings of the Zamzam springs
Illumined by the torch of a star.

& as she sings images alter within
Mosaic windows in the tomb of Akbar.

~ The opulent ink of an azure
Aurora shimmering above Kandahar.

~ The pyramids of spectral light
Imploding above ruins in Samar.

~ The circular clouds whipping
From Ararat to the straits of Shinar.

~ The steam thick as tufts of cotton
Piping from a hissing samovar.

~ The Arabian moon transforming
Into the image of Hagar.

~ The ravishing Muse whispering
Words that flow from the quill of Pindar.

~ The willows casting reflections
Of menorahs in the waters of the Isar.

~ The rushing Sarasvati
Flooding the scorched plains of Thar.

~ The Egyptian catacombs
Stalked by the shadow of a jaguar.

~ The watercolor horizon
Leaking from the brush of Renoir.

& Layla's shadow has fallen
Upon the tomb of Begum Akhtar.

In Vaikuntha turquoise suns encircle
The astral body of Begum Akhtar.

Where she meditates within an incandescent sphere.

Where she levitates above waves of frozen rivers.

Where her silhouette is emblazoned on a molten cloud.

Where her indigo shadow wavers behind a veil of light.

Where she is subsumed in the white dust of snow dervishes.

Where she hovers at the center of a myriad of birds.

Where her voice shatters the crystals of stars.

Where she is the frost of diamonds melting into rays.

Where she is the night shimmering like black sand.

Where circling falcons form a vortex around her.

Where her image undulates on a reef of celestial fire.

Where her sculptural form rises in the sky's rotunda.

*

Emerald irises bursted
From the tomb of Begum Akhtar.

A bodhi tree sprang (through silk shrouds)
From the heart of Begum Akhtar.

& particles of light teemed
In a field of swaying jowar.

& tanagers swarmed meadows
Of saxifrage in Jhalawar.

& sprigs of lightning forked
From the throne of Anshar.

& echoes thundered from the turrets
Of an ancient fortress in Salasar.

& throngs of bees rose like whirlwinds
From the ripples of hills in Jawahar.

& thunderheads sizzled with blue lightning
Above Sikh temples in Amritsar.

& glacial seas formed
From the breath of Kishar.

*

The Ganges is phosphorescent
Within the pupils of Begum Akhtar.

The Jhelum is glass populated
With reflections of Begum Akhtar.

The Sind emits fluid vapor shaping
The contours of the face of Begum Akhtar.

Her voice is Faiz's sensuous Urdu
Floating through rose gardens in Madar.

Her shadow glides above gold minarets
As moonlight whitens the roads of Chenar.

Her voice is Iqbal's ballet of words
Drifting in the silver clouds of Sagar.

Her voice the soft hum of prayers
Recited at the shrine of Zafar.

Her voice the rush of numerous linnets
In the banyan groves of Shankar.

Her voice washes over the parapets
Of the marble towers of Kadar.

Her voice spirals in the slipstream
Of a flashing jacamar.

Her voice the echo rising
From waterfalls in Barakar.

Her voice the whispering sands
Of desert isles in Kathiawar.

Her voice recites scripture carved
Into the monolith of Qarqar.

Her breath spins prayer wheels
In the monasteries of Dhankar.

Her voice an aria of air rising
Through cloud chasms in Ahaggar.

& wisps of her voice circulate in air
As a street musician plucks a sitar ~

Whirling through the smashed golds
Of wind-thrashed foliage in Srinagar.

*

Diamonds of starlit dew adorn
The tresses of Begum Akhtar.

A chinar's leaves shine like green flames
Before the spirit of Begum Akhtar.

Ghalib's lament is shaped into hymns
By the voice of Begum Akhtar.

She inhabits Kashmir zephyrs
Scented with jasmine attar.

She emanates from jade pools
In the oasis of Kashgar.

She chants Mir's lyrics as nomads
Cross the ivory dunes of Jamar.

She disperses poppies amid cenotaphs
In the ruins of Darwar.

She is resplendent rain laving
Meadows of sunflowers in Lahar.

She is the hush of cherry petals
Swirling in the orchards of Zemar.

She is an apparition of white sand
Ascending the reefs of Khobar.

She is glimpsed in mirages
Glimmering on the plains of Zaccar.

She is seen on Thakurganj road
When fog streams like steam from fresh tar.

IV

WHOM WE CALL ISHMAEL

Ghazal of Diminishment

Waves on the shore will recede & wane.
The wind's song through the reed will wane.

Rapid air rushes through its dark mane ~
But the endurance of the steed will wane.

Pressed deeply in a web of roots,
The striving of the seed will wane.

Mist quavers on a blade of grass ~
& dew, its delicate bead, will wane.

It dissolves in a galaxy's hub ~
Mortal comet whose speed will wane.

Orpheus can sing only of despair,
For love's searing need won't wane.

Cooing in cages before a pageant ~
Now, in the distance, the freed doves wane.

This body (vessel forsaking the world)
Will let the breath concede & wane.

Ghazal of the Twin Comets

In pursuit of you I left my paramour behind.
The galaxy shifted & left a star behind.

We slow danced to serenades in starlight,
But left the sounds of Ramon's guitar behind.

In our wake countries vanished at breathless speeds.
Rain sparkled on wet roads we left far behind.

You said the story we lived was ours alone
& left notes you wrote for your memoir behind.

On a whim we departed for Somaliland,
& by ship left the coast of Zanzibar behind.

We slept in pastures with bodies entwined,
But left the landscapes of Renoir behind.

My kisses dissolved in your waist ...
We entered a dream & left our bodies far behind.

You departed in the night without a farewell,
Like a comet that left its twin far behind.

Ghazal of the Elephants

(In sixth century Kashmir, Mihiragula's men
forced elephants off rock cliffs in the Pir Panjal range.)

The Hun savored the cry of falling elephants.
Did God devise the fate befalling elephants?

Songs of nomads depict their slaughter.
Peasants recite legends recalling elephants.

"Their bones like a structure, majestic in collapse ~
As if once the site of a sandstorm stalling elephants."

I recall again their story when I witness
A child, on paper, scrawling elephants.

Was it Paradise (seen in a blur)
God revealed to falling elephants?

Into a mirage they now migrate ~
Winds crossing distances, calling elephants.

Ghazal of the Startled Silence

It is the crevice a shadow crawls inside,
The cage of ribs the heart stalls inside.

It is the depths of an abyss
A stone endlessly falls inside.

An absence evolved from dimensionless Time,
The lost spaces all sound dissolves inside.

It is the maze of secret rooms
Masons built moving walls inside.

The emptiness of a pitch-black tunnel
The prisoner crawls inside.

It is the immense absence of an abandoned city,
Bombed houses the rain falls inside.

The dusty journal in an attic,
Notes the captive ghost scrawls inside.

It is the sibyl's abode, the fluttering
Dark of wind-rippled shawls inside.

Ghazal of the Black Water

Beneath trees shadows pool like black water.
Ships spin in vortexes gales fuel in black water.

Nights I pace the shore's rippled sands, watch
Circular currents unspool in black water.

When you are swept into the icy depths
Pray to dark gods who rule the black water.

Shadowy figures appear in dim moonlight
& with lances duel in black water.

Bodies plummet from a sinking freighter,
Vanish in a whirlpool of black water.

Emerging from swells in a stormy ocean,
Rapids run swift & cool through black water.

Abode of the deity who summons thunder,
Kin to storms that fuel the black water.

Ghazal of the Grasses

A fire's first sparks the wind will hone in grasses,
Igniting unheard as insects drone in grasses.

The rainbowed wings of dragonflies gleam
Amid winged-seeds sown in grasses.

Each leaf & stone meticulously fingered ~
The breeze's hands that comb the grasses.

Torn from cedars by a storm ~
Cocoons the rain has sewn to grasses.

Seagulls hectored the phantoms of mariners,
Now lulled by the dust that had blown through grasses.

A wayward dervish stalled that was compelled
Against its nature to roam the grasses.

An ocean gale raced across the shore
As if chasing sands flown from grasses.

Immersed in the rich, dark earth ~
A skull beneath its tombstone in grasses.

Ghazal of the Dust

A tornado churned like a turbine in the dust,
& left a dervish's swirling design in the dust.

The wind is polishing relics among ruins
That mark an empire's decline in the dust.

Faint whispers echoed in dissolving shadows
As a zephyr traced a line in the dust.

Spiders are etched on sunlit webs
Adorning a sultan's shrine in the dust.

Hawks descend in wide circles, gliding on
Currents of thermals that recline in the dust.

A nomad's ghost still treks the desert plains,
Whose silhouette left its outline in the dust.

Teeming with motes & specks of whirling sand,
Refracted bars of late light shine in the dust.

Entering a mirage I watched the breeze's hands
Sketch an arabesque design in the dust.

Ghazal of Death

I live wary of my death inside me.
Does Fate query my death inside me?

I bear always the weight of its presence,
Burdened to carry my death inside me.

It sleeps like grain in a husk or sometimes
Rages like the sea ~ my death inside me.

It serves as tormentor or companion
With equal facility, my death inside me.

Sometimes I'm immersed in an absence
Composed wholly of my death inside me.

It may be instilled with repose
Or roused in fury, my death inside me.

What new form will it one day
Embody, my death inside me?

My own body's prophet summoned
From within my body, my death inside me.

Houses

Houses in which bombs left empty spaces.
Their shattered mirrors haunted with faces.

You walk where there were gardens & parks,
Existing in your mind as cherished places.

Notes are whirling in a dove's throat, a song
Meant to pervade the world's darkest spaces.

You return to hear prayers recited at shrines,
As others speak of the pain only pain erases.

This where your mother's shadow billowed through
Sheets on a line ~ a memory's fleeting traces.

You are again troubled by the silence,
The dead calm in which a city braces.

Then sudden flashes of explosions.
Figures running, shadows the light chases.

& you have found refuge in a house,
Its open ceiling the rain now graces.

Memory

I conceive you now as one born of memory.
You're somewhere alive though I mourn your memory.

Their shrines destroyed, villages cling to fire.
Kashmir must bear the thorn of memory.

A dream of your mother filled with colors ~
A blur of saris worn in memory!

"Color at the edge of blood / coal of dead fires …"
Lines by Faiz held in a breath, sworn to memory.

A day's countless details are mostly lost.
Images are exiled, torn from memory.

The garden café where you'd recite Ghalib ~
Roses, red & white, adorn the memory.

The fire of the phoenix kindles the light.
Will Night, Empress of the Dark, scorn the memory?

You read ghazals to me over the phone.
Couplets left your lips to inform my memory.

Ghazal (Late at Night)

I wander streets we would walk at night,
Passing cafés where we'd talk at night.

We window-shopped ~ all signs read CLOSED ~
Storefronts on avenues we'd walk at night.

The park bench where we'd sit until daylight ...
Where winds swayed trees as we would talk at night.

Footsteps beckoned shadows to each streetlight.
We ran past alleys a ghost would walk at night.

The songs of swallows began at first light.
A silence lived in our talk at night.

The collapse of hours, the morning light.
The sound of the sea, the boardwalk at night.

I still see you in a faded light.
You whisper in my ear, we talk at night.

Broken Ghazal

Your caress made stallions doze, your hands became
Wind brushing the night's thick hair, their black manes.

From your chalet we saw locomotives weave
Through mountains, their trail of smoke across plains.

Friends write you from their fire-bombed city,
Where at night shadows dance in the shapes of flames.

Sleepless, I think of your old lovers.
As you dream your lips whisper their names.

We watched snowflakes whirl in a dervish's heart,
Flowers of frost blooming on glass panes.

You spoke of a mermaid risen from swirling
Foam, seen in the season of coastal rains.

We once sped on rails to autumnal lands.
Now clouds travel the routes of those defunct trains.

My hands memorize your hourglass waist ...
Slow winds pass through distant sands, sifting grains.

Across the Bay

A figure in black robes steers a ferry across the bay,
Through moonlit fog to an ossuary across the bay.

Fish shine like knives in lucent shallows, a seagull's
Shriek answers an echo's query across the bay.

Stone madonnas pray in a garden, rising at night
To wander ruins of a monastery across the bay.

Blown leaves scurry in a ranting wind
Laced with voices that carry across the bay.

Below an indigo ridge, fringed pines shade
The hidden grave of a mercenary across the bay.

The chanting echoes will cease only at dawn
In the ghost-infested cemetery across the bay.

Pearls adorn the hair of a mermaid, emerging
At twilight in the estuary across the bay.

A heron is incandescent in moonlight,
Whose flight is solitary across the bay.

Eye of the Storm

A plane fell like a tear from the storm's eye.
Does God decipher fear in the storm's eye?

The city braced against the wind's fury.
We saw Shiva appear in the storm's eye.

Brewing thunder, black clouds cracked open.
The lightning a spear through the storm's eye.

Debris flown through a circle's domain ~
Swirling wreckage veers towards the storm's eye.

Emptiness the center of a vortex.
Silence churns the sphere of the storm's eye.

Bodies whirled through air, sent raving
To a black frontier, through the storm's eye.

I was seized while others fled for shelter,
Trapped in the leer of the storm's eye.

Heart of the Dervish

You witnessed wind die in the heart of the dervish,
Hearing its last sigh in the heart of the dervish.

& recall fables of mystics whose spectres
Still occupy the heart of the dervish.

You have seen air roiling with seeds of unrest ~
Swirling sands that fly through the heart of the dervish.

& have requested entry into the wind's house, hearing
A zephyr's reply from the heart of the dervish.

Child of the desert, why come searching for ghosts
Whose echoes multiply in the heart of the dervish?

Then prayers were chanted by the vanished tribes,
Their voices amplify in the heart of the dervish.

You became their audience of one, & entered
As through a storm's eye the heart of the dervish.

The whispers of sages reading ancient texts
Heard in a whirlwind's cry, the heart of the dervish.

Water

A starlit bay where ghost ships sink in water.
Tonight the moon pours silver ink on water.

The gulf breezes caressed our sails,
Coursing where sunsets are pink on water.

A dead river is scorched in sand,
Where vanished tribes knelt to drink its water.

The sea is reflected in Helen's eyes ~
Blazing ships whose fires shrink in water.

Rainbows painted onto the sky's canvas ...
Brushes drain colors into a sink of water.

The night listens to a cadence of seas.
Shooting stars cast white ink on water.

Paper

Words are exiled from a country of paper,
Are burned in books, in the debris of paper.

A piano's sounds blossom in the ear …
Notes of music floating free from paper.

Men left behind mountains full of stumps.
Forests fell for a bounty of paper.

Dark waters form a pool of ink ~
The harbor for a city of paper.

Saws are buzzing like steel insects,
Turning ~ in seconds ~ a tree to paper.

Sudden sparks like uttered syllables
Ignite waves of flames in a sea of paper.

The white ink of comets trace arcs in a pond ~
A surface the moon's light turns briefly to paper.

This poem was crumpled & discarded, lifted
By the wind to swirl in a sea of paper.

The Incandescent Jacamar

Blue starlight welding the moon's scimitar.
Silver rain laving the palms of Malabar.

Fluid light in the mirrors of the Charminar.
The flight of the incandescent jacamar.

The Ganges, the Sind, the Jamuna.
The indigo shoals of Kathiawar.

Mirages shimmering like lucent mandalas
On the road to the oasis of Qarqar.

The winged dance of a ballerina's shadow
Spinning in the marble porticoes of Sennar.

A spectrum shone on bridges of vapor,
Arced above bamboo groves in Shinar.

Paisleys forming in sunlit water, arabesques
Wind-sketched in the sands of Qatar.

The note reverberating from a sitar.
The flight of the incandescent jacamar.

The night's quilt of needlepoint constellations.
White lightning woven into blue gazar.

Diamonds of starlit rain glinting
On the gold minarets of Dhankar.

Shiva materializing in heat waves
Rippling on the road to Madar.

The comet propelled from a burnished horizon.
The flight of the incandescent jacamar.

The sacred herald. The spectral dance.
The flight of the incandescent jacamar.

The evanescence. The elliptical night.
The flight of the incandescent jacamar.

The still waters. The vortex of light.
The flight of the incandescent jacamar.

The liberation. The transcendent dream.
The flight of the incandescent jacamar.

Colossal clouds. The holy enchantment.
The flight of the incandescent jacamar.

The white corona. The ecstatic dissolution.
The flight of the incandescent jacamar.

[Hornets thrum in bleached skulls wreathed in seaweed]

Hornets thrum in bleached skulls wreathed in seaweed,
Where blood-smeared sabres are sheathed in seaweed.

Nestled in black sand beneath rushing wavelets,
The sword of Achilles is sheathed in seaweed.

The prism of an aurora blazes above shoals
Beset by spectres wreathed in seaweed.

In a bonfire's shadows serpents formed of smoke
Were expelled by sparks that seethed in seaweed.

In an ocean crevasse the ruins of Atlantis
Are patrolled by furies wreathed in seaweed.

As beached galleons burned on Samos, fallen coins
Glowed like embers that seethed in seaweed.

[Within the eyes of dying djinns tunnels]

Within the eyes of dying djinns tunnels
Of light like vaulted corridors dissolve.

Lightning sizzles above cobalt mountains
As veils of fog on frozen moors dissolve.

Immersed in the flood tides of a surging
Ocean, phosphorescent shores dissolve.

Light bursts in sieves through lucent clouds
In which flocks of soaring condors dissolve.

Shadows liquefy into pools of black water ~
Mirrors in which the moon's contours dissolve.

Comets careen through a pulsing aurora,
Convulsing as their icy cores dissolve.

[Circe once bathed in a cove between the sandy cliffs]

Circe once bathed in a cove between the sandy cliffs,
Now a rock-strewn waste jackals rove between the sandy cliffs.

Seaweed veils gold wheels from chariots
Odysseus drove between the sandy cliffs.

Sibyls cross a bridge of lightning that streams
From the scepter of Jove, between the sandy cliffs.

Maps encrypted in cave murals guide wayfarers through
Barren passes demons rove between the sandy cliffs.

Vines swarm the gate of an untended garden, voices linger
In gusts scented with moly & clove between the sandy cliffs.

A gargoyle sentry is perched in a ridge's cleft
Like an Angel sheltered in an alcove, between the sandy cliffs.

Windy abode of falcons that plucked snakes from the sea,
Shrieked as they circled & dove between the sandy cliffs.

Nereids & dolphins leap in streaming fog ~ an ocean
Tapestry moonlight wove between the sandy cliffs.

Gales harrow the abandoned temple of Circe, whose shadow
Shimmers on the rock walls of a cove between the sandy cliffs.

Sand

Water erased words I printed in sand.
Shells are bleached & newly minted in sand.

Within the wind a sound of endlessness.
The air whirled & sprinted through sand.

Caravans trek a starving desert,
Vanish in waves of sun-tinted sand.

Light Streams Through the Stained Glass Madonna

Light streams through the stained glass Madonna,
Becomes a shimmering prism as She rises
Within the Transcendent world anew.

The cathedral ceiling a cloudy vortex
With white doves gliding amid Tiepolo's saints,
Rising within the Resplendent world anew.

St. Teresa recites *The Devotions of Ecstasy*,
Entranced as she levitates immersed in light ~
Rising within the Ascendent world anew.

Of Blue & Gold

The mirrors that shimmered
As Radha's saris blazed blue & gold.

The Oracle's voice whispering
From sacred vases glazed blue & gold.

The pulsing suns of Andromeda
Fiery comets grazed, blue & gold.

The distant fires of cities
Alexander razed, blue & gold.

The windy caverns with shadows
Of djinns that blazed blue & gold.

The gleaming horizons studded
With stars that blazed blue & gold.

The meteor showers like crystal rain
In nebulas that blazed blue & gold.

Shahid's vision of burning mountains
Twilit smoke hazed blue & gold.

Ghazal Considering the Composition of a Sonnet

The rain threads air, listens to its own
Measured sound & sews it in a sonnet.

Pushkin stole the breath of Siberia
& froze it in a sonnet.

In Paradise Milton nurtures the creative seed
& grows it in a sonnet.

Michaux spoke of worlds hidden inside the world
& disguised a crisp prose within a sonnet.

Shelley heard the ocean breeze whisper rumors of storms,
& wrote of the enchantments of death's repose in a sonnet.

Petrarch portrays an armada of ships rushing to the horizon ~
Fashioned in the cadence to which an oarsman rows, in a sonnet.

God's name rises in calligraphy from Tagore's palm,
Amid mountains shrouded in whirling snows ~ in a sonnet.

Millay's descriptive walks through dark coves ~ the wind
Whispering through a stir of echoes, in a sonnet.

I gaze at windows bent in a wine glass, depicting
How each reflected cloud becomes a rose, in a sonnet.

Ghazal of the Sacred Ground

The night's dark wrapped its cloak around me.
From every direction voices spoke around me.

I had sought to pass this place in silence
When an ocean of wind broke around me.

Here the turmoil of the past remains.
Dead fires emit their smoke around me.

Did I wake you, dark god? What intent
Compels the spirits you evoke around me?

They slept for centuries hidden in cold
Crypts, but suddenly woke around me.

Lord, grant me means to repel spectres
I unwittingly provoke around me.

I see a battle's aftermath, heads raised
On lances ~ their voices swirl like smoke around me.

May this be but a dream that vanishes
& sleep wrap a silent cloak around me.

Ghazal of the Belovéd

How often had he walked
Beneath summer and the sky
To receive her shadow in his mind ...
~ Wallace Stevens

With what blessing does God grace the Belovéd?
By what star's course may we trace the Belovéd?

What site ~ divine sepulcher or holy tomb ~
May we honor, call the place of the Belovéd?

Voice preserved in the ear, image in the mind ...
From memory will Time erase the Belovéd?

Who sought her exile from the world,
Banished from mirrors the face of the Belovéd?

Her silhouette is seen in the twilight clouds,
Thought night arrives to displace the Belovéd.

A field of ashes where embers were dying,
Light by which we strove to retrace the Belovéd.

Her presence now constitutes the hush between
Prayers ~ the sacred space of the Belovéd.

The defunct monastery still covets silence,
Where priests saw an Angel embrace the Belovéd.

Ghazal Spoken by Rumi

All grief is born outside of silence.
Let sorrows dissolve, subside in silence.

You sing, releasing birds from your throat ~
Melodies that glide towards silence.

Words form in the spilled ink of shadows,
Amid secrets we confide to silence.

The world shrinks suddenly from your touch
& you're beckoned by your guide, the silence.

Within a seed the flower's form is preconceived.
Thoughts engender an image, abide in silence.

Asked of the nature of Creation's essence,
Siddhartha had replied with silence.

What is abiding cannot be reduced,
Just silence when one divides the silence.

Let the space between your thoughts widen.
Listen for God in a tide of silence.

Watch the thorns bud into roses ...
I, Rumi, speak from inside the silence.

Through Spirals of a Seashell

Through spirals of a seashell a hurricane advances,
Like wind in tunnels through which a train advances.

In a chalk-white chapel with varnished pews, rosaries
Are uttered as the chorus of the rain advances.

Burnt hills at dusk, slight blades of spinning leaves ~
As a scything wind through fields of grain advances.

A disciple to his guiding ghost ~ behind you
In a mirror the image of Montaigne advances.

Notes of music are whirling in a vortex of wind,
As a symphony of leaves through a darkened lane advances.

Heat waves above dunes evolve to dancing flames ~
Toward a mirage of palms the fiery terrain advances.

Bolts of lightning are oars rowing fast clouds,
As the flood rising in the Seine advances.

Ghazal of Restoration

The bitterness you harbor wanes tonight.
No strife within you remains tonight.

No dervish will trouble the dust.
No tornado ravages the plains tonight.

No bright flak, no disputed barricades.
The wars have ended their campaigns tonight.

All sleep. None long for departure.
Stations have only idle trains tonight.

You lived in prisons of your own making.
The captive heart dissolves its chains tonight.

From deserts a paradise will emerge.
Parched lands are blessed with rains tonight.

You dream of Eden, when the animals appear ~
& listen as Adam recites their names tonight.

A hush. Silence is now the world's prayer.
From God's hand stars fall like grains tonight.

In memory of Norma Horstmann (1914-2006)

Japanese Ghazal

The fragrance of chrysanthemums in a tea house ~
Through paper walls a geisha's shadow bows.

*

Sunlit water beneath Saihoji temple ~ in a minnow's
Transparent body the diminutive heart pulses.

*

A tempest stitched into the fabric of the sea ~
Lightning in the clouds of Banzaemon's kimono.

*

Stone lanterns breached by swarming moths ~ a path
Through grass lit by the brief torches of wings.

*

Air swirls in catacombs of a desiccated bee hive,
Branches of an ancient gingko tree caging the breeze.

*

Its dark glass reflects Eguchi in brocaded silk,
The mirror by day embodied as a pond.

*

Zen priests rake gravel, shaping waves that evoke
The sensation of a deafening surf upon rocky islands.

*

Water drips into a puddle, the only sound
In The Palace of the Bodhisattvas.

*

A forest's memory of ashes falling like black snow ...
The phoenix's vacant nest in an Empress tree.

*

At Taga castle turtles are kept in wooden buckets,
Awaiting release in the marshes as karmic offerings.

*

Lady Sarashina depicts her trek through mountain passes,
A galloping calligraphy wrought in austere black.

*

Issa listens for poems in the wind's exhalations,
Likens koans to tangled wisteria vines.

*

The spell of wind-chimes sounding at Ise shrine ~
A tree frog poised in the bamboo leaf's basin of dew.

*

The sun's red disc dissolves in the ocean ...
Twilight's jewel ~ a single, loitering star.

*

Kizan dreams a silent funnel cloud rising above water,
Hears the sea whisper into the ear's shell.

*

Beneath Mt. Fuji a pavilion's bell tolls,
Cherry blossoms falling on a samurai's shrine.

*

A grove of candles surrounds a Shinto altar,
Tongues of light flickering without voices.

*

Bashō sips hot saki in the temple at Suma beach ~
The ebony ocean studded with the duplicates of stars.

The World Your Word Kept Between Us

Tell me of the world your word kept between us ~
Of our strife, like sudden flames that leapt between us.

Tell me of what lay dormant, in our bed
A body of silence that slept between us.

A disturbance billowed drapes in the vacant chambers,
Revealed as a ragged shadow that crept between us.

You saw notes of music whirling in the air,
A symphony of leaves the wind swept between us.

Tell me of what lingered for years without being spoken of,
The phantom in our room that wept between us.

Tell me of the word that quivered in your breath,
That took shape as a presence & stepped between us.

We sleep, we wind ourselves in cool sheets.
Tell me of the world your word kept between us.

[In Jahanara's chandeliered boudoir]

In Jahanara's chandeliered boudoir,
Diamond laced shawls & silk brocades shine.

Glazing Mt. Fuji's iced slopes,
Hiroshige's ivory cascades shine.

Encircled by yews & dense buckthorn,
Glengarriff's sea-green glades shine.

With black light from an onyx moon,
Mount Mazama's palisades shine.

On Abu Simbel's star-lit facade
Nefertari's ebony braids shine.

Chagall's Madonnas, in a spectrum
Of stained-glass shades, shine.

With candescent Marian apparitions,
Deir el-Bersha's colonnades shine.

Coils of barbed-wire skirting
Verdun's barricades shine.

Snared in nets, thrashing mackerel
Like steel blades shine.

A typhoon's silver lightning bolts,
Like damascened blades, shine.

Gold sunbeams streaming through
Rome's vaulted arcades shine.

Flanked by war chariots, Qin Shi Huang's
Terracotta brigades shine.

[In a temple hall Cleopatra's crystal casket shines]

In a temple hall Cleopatra's crystal casket shines.
The lavender mist that shrouds a budding violet shines.

Beads of rain absorbing moonlight become diamonds.
Frosted dew on the feathery palms of Gilgit shines.

The night is a steed Abbas rides to the Euphrates ~
Where Gula's spectre, oarsman of The Prophet, shines.

A scribe's deft stylus glides on parchment,
Where by firelight his credo in Sanskrit shines.

Mystical Rose, Our Lady of the Candelabra ~
Crowned with a halo in a stained glass portrait, shines.

An emerald sky becomes the night's spectral dust.
The white flame of each comet in transit shines.

Dusk's fiery glint on the Brazilian Sea, in stone
Cristo Redentor on Corcavado's summit shines.

Sambethe chants sutras, invoking Brahma, Vishnu, Shiva ~
The Vedic trinity engraved in her amulet shines.

Father, my lament is veiled in a Eucharistic hymn.
The light you departed your body to inhabit shines.

Ghazal of Departure

This is a silence ravaged with despair,
A state of anguish which to pray in.

I mine the darkness, extract its essence ~
Shards of time for the world to decay in.

You were a butterfly dreaming yourself a man,
Given a cocoon of light to stay in.

We kindled fires, the dancing flames
Emitted light for their shadows to sway in.

I drew charcoal trees beneath a blank sky.
You penciled slanting rain & sketched the gray in.

Rooms listen to the guitar's chord fade,
Denying it an echo to play in.

Our boat sailed a milky coast of stars,
Departed the dream we spent the day in.

I watched a nebula vanish ~
The cloud of light you drifted away in.

You Are Leaving

You turn to view the city you are leaving ~
Above which your plane is a moving star, leaving.

Through the world you are pursued by many
Who have only seen you from afar, leaving.

Yours is a love cannot long be possessed.
No farewell or last kiss to mar your leaving.

You were observed on a train (writing in
A journal notes for your memoir), leaving.

I saw by chance a glimpse of your face
In the blur of a passing car, leaving.

There were rumors of your death in some
Distant country which now you are leaving.

You move through the din of city streets
& vanish in crowds at Shahran Bazaar, leaving.

One day, it is said, you will be destitute.
Hurtling through the night in a boxcar, leaving.

& even now you are stepping out of this page ~
To the sound of a hissing samovar, leaving.

Ghazal of Departure (A Reprise)

A precise moment one may properly sigh in ~
Before a prayer meant to silently cry in.

I am walking down a hall of mirrors
In which your reflections multiply in.

The sound of my footsteps dying in an alley ...
Your stifled call inviting a passerby in.

You wrote of mariners asleep in tombs of water.
I hold a shell one hears the sea's lullaby in.

This is a silence ravaged with despair, making
Me long for the crypt I will finally lie in.

Sunlight streamed through a cocoon
I saw a sleeping butterfly in.

You stepped like Elijah into a whirlwind
Powerful enough to rein the sky in.

Ghazal

Rumi became a sage for us.
Ghalib's ghazals revealed an age to us.

A poem was written with moonlight,
Deftly inscribed on a pond's page for us.

We were heirs to a kingdom of dust.
You foretold wars the world would wage for us.

Banished to the desert without water,
The storms you summoned would rage for us.

In a dream we were birds perched on a branch.
Shadows built in the trees a cage for us.

You are composed now completely of light.
O the world was your theatre, a stage for us.

Ghalib's Ghost

In whispers Ghalib read verse to you.
For years his ghost conversed with you.

To an empty room you'd recite ghazals ~
Your voice wove in air words rehearsed by you.

We'd rest on blankets of wrinkled shadows,
Assessing the darkness traversed by you.

A poet's domain is a sea of words.
Who could save one so immersed as you?

In a parched voice you sang a desert song,
Implying nothing could slake the thirst in you.

Your parting words were for *her* alone ~
Your mother the Muse prompting verse from you.

The room was deafened, silence your shroud.
The light left your eyes, dispersed from you.

They are the great mentors ~ Ghalib, Rumi, Hafiz ~
Whose words I heard recited first by you.

Broken Ghazal

We're inside the fire, looking for the dark.
~ Agha Shahid Ali

Nights you leaned above a pond's black mirror,
Waiting for the moonlight to etch your face within it.

In my dream your shadow moves through a lit corridor,
Rushing away to leave no trace within it.

I close my eyes & hear your voice ~ the prayer
You'd recite simply to consider the grace within it.

Wavering reflections melded in wind-rippled water.
You saw the arms of temples & mosques embrace within it.

I stand like an exclamation mark in a cemetery of snow,
Envisioning the shrine of words I'll place within it.

Above the Himalayas the sky became spectral dust,
As you witnessed comets teem & race within it.

This is your broken ghazal, fleeting words
The wind's breath will encase within it.

Shahid, you're inside the fire, searching for the dark ~
Having returned to claim a space within it.

Whom We Call Ishmael

Here there are ghosts none can repel tonight.
Rumors of the world's end none can dispel tonight.

In prisons the executions are beginning.
One hears prayers spoken from each cell tonight.

The enemy now approaches our city.
What outcome did the Oracle foretell tonight?

They are now among us, those demons
Who departed for Earth from Hell tonight.

In the temple only shadows bow in worship ~
Without a priest to toll its knell tonight.

Tornadoes curve in descent, pulling down
A sky from which archangels fell tonight.

A moonlit terrace above deafened streets
Awaits the silhouette of Jezebel tonight.

You were comforted by the evening star, shining
Like a brilliant coin in the sacred well tonight.

We search for him whose words have guided us ~
The Belovéd ~ whom we call Ishmael tonight.

ACKNOWLEDGEMENTS

Thanks to friends and family members who have supported me in the writing of these ghazals, including, in particular, Rebecca Byrkit, Antonia Alexandra Klimenko, Gudrun Langille, Brenda Lyons, Jane Reichhold, Werner Reichhold, Diana Rowles, Anja Spangenberg, and R.W. Watkins.

My heartfelt thanks, also, to Dylan Spangenberg, for his meticulous and unflagging help with this manuscript.

It is with deep gratitude to my remarkable teachers I acknowledge Agha Shahid Ali and Jon Anderson, who are greatly missed and who remain in my thoughts always.

I want to express my everlasting gratitude to the late Gene Doty (1941-2015), for his scrupulous reading, advice and support, and his sage friendship through the years. Gene wrote the Foreword for *Jalsaghar* in the summer of 2013.

With love to my sons Nathan, Ryan, and Jonathan.

*   *   *

I would like also to take this opportunity to acknowledge *The Ghazal Page* (now edited by Holly Jensen) and *Lynx* (edited by Jane and Werner Reichhold), online journals that have ~ since the 90's, and continuing to this day ~ supported the development of the ghazal in English.

My grateful appreciation also goes out to R.W. Watkins, editor and publisher of *Contemporary Ghazals*, the only print journal dedicated exclusively to ghazals written in English.

ABOUT THE AUTHOR

Steffen Horstmann was born in Niskayuna, New York, and attended the University of Arizona. As Agha Shahid Ali's student, he studied the history of the ghazal form and began writing his own ghazals in English. Horstmann's poems and book reviews have appeared in publications throughout the world, including *Baltimore Review*, *Free State Review*, *Istanbul Literary Review*, *Louisiana Literature*, *Oyez Review*, *Texas Poetry Journal*, and *Tiferet*. He resides in Naples, Florida.

Praise for Steffen Horstmann's

Jalsaghar

"Steffen Horstmann's *Jalsaghar* renews in English the enduring power and lyricism of the ancient ghazal. His is a voice echoing the elegant rhythms of Agha Shahid Ali. This new collection is historically attuned and deeply rooted in Hindu and Urdu literary traditions. A stunning achievement."
　–Brenda Lyons

"Steffen Horstmann's ability to follow the traditional requisites of the ghazal form while at the same time creating modern poetry in English is something many people have said could not be done. With his book, *Jalsaghar*, he marvelously proves them wrong. His amazing feat in using old patterns to make new poetry suggests a past life bleed-through."
　–Jane Reichhold, Co-editor of *Lynx*

"Steffen Horstmann's ghazals illuminate the form's potential in English."
　–Gene Doty, Editor of *The Ghazal Page*

Printed in the United States
By Bookmasters